About the Author

Jamie is an entrepreneur, having owned and managed many companies in an eclectic mix of entertainment and retail areas, from restaurants and a chain of clothes shops, to nightclubs and theatres across the whole of London. He currently resides in the heart of the Northamptonshire countryside, where he has been able to explore the interior rhythms of a lifetime spent in practicing and teaching the ancient martial art of Tai Chi, and reflecting inwardly on his changing emotions throughout this incredible life.

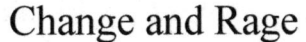
Change and Rage

Jamie Bloom

Change and Rage

Vanguard Press

VANGUARD PAPERBACK

© Copyright 2023
Jamie Bloom

Front cover photo credits: Wolfgang Mustain

The right of Jamie Bloom to be identified as author of
this work has been asserted by them in accordance with the
Copyright, Designs and Patents Act 1988.

All Rights Reserved

No reproduction, copy or transmission of this publication
may be made without written permission.
No paragraph of this publication may be reproduced,
copied or transmitted save with the written permission of the
publisher, or in accordance with the provisions
of the Copyright Act 1956 (as amended).

Any person who commits any unauthorised act in relation to
this publication may be liable to criminal
prosecution and civil claims for damages.

A CIP catalogue record for this title is
available from the British Library.

ISBN 978 1 80016 886 2

*Vanguard Press is an imprint of
Pegasus Elliot Mackenzie Publishers Ltd.*
www.pegasuspublishers.com

First Published in 2023

**Vanguard Press
Sheraton House Castle Park
Cambridge England**

Printed & Bound in Great Britain

To my gorgeous wife Joanne, who encouraged me to begin this journey, reflecting on my past to improve my present.

Acknowledgements

I would like to thank Hayley Davies without whose hard work, continued support and enthusiasm, this book would not have made it into print.

THINGS HAVE CHANGED

Chalk on the blackboards
Ink, italic nibs, caps
Short trousers
Six of the best
Coloured bus tickets
Gobstoppers, sherbet dip,
You're never alone with a Strand,
Tobacco that counts - Marlboro Man
Tobacco that doesn't - Consulate
Gitanes for the cool!
Minis, Cortinas, E types - so fast
Now you would be last.
Flares, bell bottoms, boas and beads
Flowers in your hair and Afghan coats
Reefers, not coats, furnished flats
Equipped with roaches, whatever kind
Sex and the pill and then the clap,
Road maps, phone boxes (that worked)
Shillings and pence
All so lax, nearly no tax
Elvis and Beatles, Stones and stoned
It was a great time, slower pace
Snake skin boots and belts
Now it's so fast,
as long as we don't have a power blackout
then it won't last.
The time of our lives to be young and so free
A time of love and peace
with a rather short lease.

LOVE

I love you,
but do you love me?
I love you tonight
but maybe not in the morning…

I love cake, crumpets, my dog, my cat, my hat,
a misused word
love is everywhere and nowhere
does it last?
Or just transient, ephemeral
love grows or does it dilute?

The passion, the lust, the desire
both gain everything with each new climax
only to become vulnerable to one another again,
when you lose your house, your money, your kids,
Is that love?
True love?

Songs about love, but also the blues
cheating affairs, dark love,
love you always, or maybe not…
Maybe shut up
And accept the lot.

DAYS

Wakes up
Nervous, thinking…
What could go wrong today?
Small things, blown up
Insurance, tax, debts, bets,
shares up or down?
It is early, unreal
Sweaty, panic
Had a bad dream, racing, chasing
So gloomy, so negative
Is it me?
Need some tea
All so hazy, going crazy
Now hang on mate
It is not so late
Becoming clear,
Its only fear
Early morning blues
Where're my fucking shoes?

HEROES

Dogs are heroes, they always listen
never argue back
They are loyal and friendly and always there when life
    is hitting back
They lie with you when you're asleep
and guard your every move
They wag, no brag
living just for you
they don't want much
just love and tickles while lying on their backs

But sometimes cast away, abandoned on the tracks
How can people do this?
They should be treasured
Your fine friends
Heroes of our time.

DOGGIES

They bound at you
Jumping and licking
Sniffing and snuffling
What a greeting, what a treat,
Unconditional love
Furry friends
Little black noses
Happy eyes
Throw my ball
That is all.

BREAKFAST

It's nice to have an egg
So oval, so smooth, so perfect
Toast and Jam
Tea for me
Best meal of the day
My way.

THE WAY

The way, the Tao, this journey
Spiral energy, rotating, the tan tien;
To where we know not.
With every breath, falling into a vortex
Of self-realisation, self-confrontation
Flying with the soul,
Fajing in my hands and my body.
One inch power, single trip, single whip,
Transforming with every step.
The easy is not simple.
Yielding to overcome all attacks verbal,
Internal, invisible, magic ghostly,
Fading into stillness
Making all a meditation, not a vexation, to the spirit.

Mama's boys the yin, the feminine, all in the black
A complete circle and back to crossing hands.
Crossing lands.
Tai Chi, the fantastic voyage to all unknown
Yet opening to the known.
Blind man tapping on his way to the Tao
Redirecting the trajectory with gentle touch.
When the key fits, the shoe's on not forced,
Spinning, spiralling into the emptiness
Falling with perfect balance, going unnoticed
Breathing easily, avoiding extremes.
Economy of energy, worry is pointless, give up:
Let it happen, confront with softness
Learning the extraordinary.
Beyond understanding.

FOOLS' LAUGHTER

Knowing nothing is useful when learning
Nothing to compare it to - no history
Now you can learn
Being empty, an open vessel
Like entering the fool's laughter
The moves, the dance, the way, the ray, the light
Connecting, advancing, clear direction, yielding
A time of flowing, knowing who you are and who you could be
Floating and falling into the void
Total fulfilment, desiring nothing
Nowhere to go, nothing to show
Just being, walking
the path, the way.
It's worth a try, worth a go.

REGRET

Dilemma is but part of me
As I sit here and think
I wish I was an animal
About to leave my link
I feel as though you might be here
Alone with me today
And then it's not me at all
It's you who's gone away

Soul drifting over hill
Mind so far away, feelings I can't comprehend
Do come and fall away
To know the truth of life and death
Please come back today.

WHO AM I?

How to know who you are
conditioned as kids
playing with boys
playing with toys
Who am I?

Do I follow the cash…
Or follow my dream?
Do what I want
Do what I need

Life is short
75 summers if we're lucky
Should I do what I feel…
Or stay on the wheel?

To pursue the grind
Or see what I find

Having no voice
having no choice
can't dismount
Be the rider, stay on the tiger
Owe a lot, can't get off
So who am I?

Do I want to be free?
Do I want to be me?
Do I need responsibility?
Wives and kids
then we're trapped,
stuck on a rail, in our own jail
Should I retire, or stay on the wire
Or get off this track?
Be my own man
Do what I can
Easier times, not down in the mine
Life without lines

Such a fleeting look, such a short book
I'm all alone now out, without a bow
Be true to myself
If I can!
If I know who I am.

TIME

Branches reaching out to me
Sea - so still and calm
Sun so high, so bright, so warm
Sits proudly in the sky
As time drifts slowly by,
People walk and talk so loud
But never see what's passing by.

Playing, thinking, contemplating
Waiting for a chance,
Hoping, scheming, never blinking
Averting every glance
Knowing that a moments' signal
could cut you like a lance,
Time is going, time is reaching
Stretching for the moon
Fading into oblivion
Like a song without a tune.

MUGGED

The blow came from nowhere as if I was not there
My knees began to crumble my head was full of
nothing, distracted and confused.
I was mugged alone I should have been more careful,
not playing on my phone.
My eyes began to open bruised and painful
nothing more to see nothing to hang onto only you
You and me.
You and me.

ANONYMITY

I'm on my way
Lightened by load, on the road
No text, no email, no phone,
On my own, towards my safe cell, cabin
On the island; no power, wood fires
Anonymity, can't be reached, cannot be found
No address, don't exist, a place to hide
No stress, no strife, no bills

A womb, a cave, just my dog for company
Away from it all, no bullshit
Maybe I'll stay here
Lie on the earth, back to my birth
No questions, no answers, no decisions
Time to be,
Unknown, distant, free!
Change my name
Being, seeing, unreachable
Nobody knows where I am, great; safe
For now.
My refuge from the cruel world
She's tranquil, peaceful
My little home
She's part wood so she breathes
Life from the flowing river
But most of all, nobody knows where.

AGEING

We all get old
All decay
Cannot think straight
Lose our way
We trip and fall
Stiffen up
Our looks recede as time impedes
It slips away, picks up speed
Lose our keys, can't find our cars
Find ourselves in some old bar
Who am I now?
What do I think?
Lost myself, can't find the sink
But no one there, or cares
It slips away, another day
Another year, another fear

INSIDE

I feel there's something in me,
Things that do not fill
Tills and bills and wills
I wonder what went wrong
But nothing lasts forever
Nothing lasts for long.
It's life with all its edges
Sharpen but blunt the light
Make you feel uneasy
Robs you of the fight.

POETRY

Don't say a word
Its a literary work
Poetry is all it is
Words set right
Eyeing the door
Watching the floor
Wanting to stop
Needing belief
A beggar and a thief
Stopping my brain
Halting thoughts
Connecting words
Look at the birds
Can't see the sky
Wonder why?
Don't know my name
Can't play the game
Need to be there
To find words that
resonate with you
A cathartic time
that doesn't rhyme
It's all getting clear,
coming near
To end this day
in an alternative way

To weep, to sleep
To dream again in bars
touch the stars
Scan the pages
Champing at the bit
Nothing lit, nothing fits
Dark and gloomy
Losing the plot
To hell with the lot!

CASH

Worrying about money,
Cash, dosh
High inflation, gas and electric bills
Tax and keeping your job
Paying the bill, writing your will
A bill for everyday
There's more, council tax
Insurance, car and life and kids,
paying for your teeth
On the treadmill
It never ends, new kitchen
car, HP and finance
mortgages and more
hang on to the house
foods and eating out
having fun, it all costs money
we work then we die
and more taxes, more bills
how good it would be
to sit under a tree, jump off
a bottle of wine
that would be fine
free as a bird
not even a word.

YES

Say yes, say yes
Not no, not no
Yes changes everything
Hotwires, inspires
Don't say no - have a go
Say yes, say yes.
A three-letter word can change your life,
change your mind
Say yes, say yes.
It's all it takes
A different road to just unload
Say yes, say yes!

SIRENS

Lying in bed
sirens running through my head
Thoughts whirling, often red
Pattern of work, ebbing and flowing
sirens running through my head

Sounds, merry-go-rounds
that pound inside my brain
infused with love and pain

Upon waking, no sirens, no rain
equilibrium at last, no past
went to hell, no tales to tell
Spiralling down the well
now some peace, so serene
down the street
level feet.
New day to meet.

IF

If things go wrong
It won't be long
Time will fly
Lets say goodbye
Moving on
Staying strong

If only when
If only then
Time will read
Time will speed
We can't go on
We won't survive
If there's no light
If nothing's right

As time goes by
If we live a lie
If it's all hard work
There is no point
Just carry on
When all goes wrong.

DARKER

At times she wants it darker,
sometimes harder,
or holding hands,
light, but dark, thought-
provoking, stirring, not love,
a paradox of love and hate.

She states I lie,
I try, as best I can.
calls me a vampire,
one foot in the shadows
an evil ride, a wicked plan?

Criticises, fantasises
Drama personified.
A fevered climax
of her play
A ray of hope
could be dope
But around the table
the dope is me.

It's her plea, she wants it all
to be alive, thrive
but looking for aggro
wanting the facts alone.

Insecure desires,
perfection needs protection
only to grate and gnash
ties you up with her red sash
tightens the knot,
just gets darker,
closes the latch,
bolts the door,
makes you sore,
makes you squirm
you're my worm,
having a lark
leaving you standing in the dark.

TOLD

Doing what I'm told, can't break the mould,
Can't change my way
Can't change the day
Can't integrate,
Don't follow rules,
Don't have the tools

Feel my struggle, carry on
Doing what I'm told
Found my voice,
Made my choice
Along the road
All the way
Another day, it's what I do
It's how I move
Take some risks
Make some waves
It's all a joke

Tried it straight
It's now too late
Cannot retreat
Or even cheat
The dark is light
The light is night
Can't be told

Can't break the mould

Feeling good
Feeling right
I can fight, I can sing
Play guitar and make it ring
all in tune
Breaking rules
They're all fools!
All so lost
Out of reach, out of touch
All in a mess
All a test.

MIGHT

You might be light
You might be up all night
You might be all alone
You might be away at sea
You might be here with me
You might be about to fail
You might be about to change
You might be on the stage
You might be on time
You might be without a dime
You might be a winner
You might be a loser
You might be strong
You might be wrong
You might be a lover
You might be on a cover
You might be full of anger
You might be full of peace
You might be a poet
You might work in a shop
You might write a flop
You might get to the top
You might have a look
You might write a book
You might sweep streets
Who knows what you'll be
But does it really matter?
Let's just wait and see.

WORRY

Worry is pointless
It does no good
Drains your energy
Changes nothing
Makes you tremble and sweat
Guilt as well does nothing
You can't sleep with it
Eats you up
Only confronting things,
Dealing with them
Making decisions makes a difference.
Make a choice, have a voice
Do something, anything
Face it, look it in the eyes
Drop the lies, then it defuses
Life goes on
No time for worry, waste of time
Get up and go
Move on, loosen the load on the road.
Decisions change it all, break the wall,
Ease the fall.

SOUL FORCE

The garden, the land
Flavours of life - lavender, lily, oak, and lime
Earth enriches your time
Creatures - squirrels, worms even rats,
Bats and bees
All busy with their seeds
Such a meditation,
Lost in rhyme,
Lost in time.

THE OTHER SIDE OF MIDNIGHT

It was the other side of midnight
I had to go to work
To greet and meet and be polite
When you couldn't hear a word

It was the other side of midnight
When most are sound asleep
I had to drive there tired
Sit there on my own
Surrounded by people,
Yet sitting alone.

It was the other side of midnight
It all became so boring
Everyone distracted on the phone
Wishing they weren't there
But this was not to be.

It was the other side of midnight
So much tack
An empty pit of nothing
A mirror painted black.

LAST

I knew it couldn't
It was all too fast
The cash, the cars and bars,
Boats and planes
Vast
It couldn't last
It tumbled down
It's in the past.

THE GAME

You're right, I'm right
Who dares, who cares?
It just goes on
Not for long
Lies and ties
In the bowl, in a hole
No one dares
No one cares
A load of strife
Waste of life
In or out, does it matter?
It is all the same
Just a game.

MOVING FAST

Time has moved so quickly
Where has it all gone?
I was once so young and vibrant
It seemed so far, so long
Old friends have all departed
Mum and Dad and Lol

But does it really matter?
It went at such a rate
Before it's all ended
Before they close the gate.

THE YEAR

It was a tough year,
Brexit, Covid, Omicron
Shops closed, little income,
confusion going to live, going to die
does it matter?
Something will end this life
This strife, the final exit

But wait,
it's easing, feels short lived
Hey! life goes on,
this is such a fleeting existence
which experiences the material
but on the way to the spiritual it's a one-way ticket
Or maybe not,nobody's come back from the trip
The final slip
Maybe it's a holiday.

So, we plod on with
whatever burdens we drag with us
Rocks on our backs labelled with our personal faults
Maybe if we really knew it, it would all be pointless,
The earning, the grabbing, the accumulation, the homes,
Mortgages, dishwashers, kitchens, garden furniture,
cash on deposit, if you are lucky, bitcoins cyber,
all the get rich quick shit, once it was all free

fruit, fire, fish
What we need, what we want are so different
Wait and see
It's coming, like it or not,
it's a glimpse
All borrowed,
all left behind.

MARRIAGE

A compromise at best
Ignore the rest
Accusing eyes
So many lies
So many ties
Would love to be free
Only to flee
But time marches on
no lawyer would agree
too open-ended
Always extended
But would it matter another
Woman, a new relationship
Will it bear my name?
We keep on trying
To make things better
But can you work all day
And work when you stay?
But we all play the game
Or get a divorce.
Released from the wrench
Back on the bench
They must have your back
Or stay on the rack.
It's so bloody hard
To be the perfect man
takes empathy and skill
A force of the will.

FREEDOM

The open fields so full of life
Do call me every day
To smell the grass so fresh and cold
It takes my breath away
I love this place, with all its moods
 it's not the way back there
So I'll just sit and fly away
My thoughts no longer here.

THE CAT'S DILEMMA

I'm upstairs, I'm downstairs
I'm coming in and out
I'm falling, I'm rising
I'm turning all about
Come here, go there
The mouse did rant
The day has just begun.

Cat moved slowly
He didn't want to fight
He knew what he was thinking
So not to give to fright
You know me as I know you
Could you please come in?
No, my head's too big
Get out; not here
That's in.

POLARITY

Are you bad?
Or are you good?
You don't love me
As you should.

Do you care?
Are you fair?
You cannot see me
Only through your ego
Let me go
Or let me stay,
Between these two poles I sway

You don't love me
As I love you
Might be true,
Or maybe not.

All my empathy
You're psychotic
Situation chaotic
You strain my nerves
Bending the curves
As I struggle to comprehend.

TIME STOOD STILL

The square in the south
motorbikes everywhere
ancient and medieval
donkeys look so sad
packs of dogs lead the way
snake charmers and monkeys
Time stood still

Thousands of stalls
similar stuff
but happy enough
those who had nothing but
the shirt on their backs
took me to somewhere
I have been before
out on the streets
serving and selling all at a price
Heat of the day, scent and smells
sounds of the Mosques
affect the soul
Yet time stood still
Spend time with Latiffe
A man of no lies.
Look into my eyes!
A man or a thief
but no ordinary man

A man of great depth
I knew who I was
A moment in time

As we spoke of philosophy
of writers and rhyme
We were two strangers
who shared a short time
but was he a thief
Now just relief.

GLASS HALF EMPTY

I've had enough of people
with complaints
They are fault-finders, sidewinders
nothing hits, nothing fits
The shoes are much too small
key doesn't fit the lock
Oh, what a shock!
Finding faults, finding flaws
having nothing else to do
Lucky they are not in Ukraine
In the driving rain
with missiles flying overhead
not moaning in their bed
Maybe it's not the room
but the owning of their gloom
Everything is now reviewed
being true or false
But fault-finding is what they like
what they have to do
But hey, is it you?

THE BEGINNING

"Hello ladies, they're all cheap today,"
"How much is this, how much is that?"
They were such fun days
Dresses and coats, that's what we sold
"I can't buy that, how will I feed my old man?"
"Don't worry about his dinner or telling him lies
He won't be very hungry, he will eat you with his eyes."
You will look so sexy, without any blag,
Hang on a minute, I'll put it in a bag."

It only got better,
Sometimes much wetter
Cash in my pockets, cash in my jeans
I was richer than ever
More than I'd ever been,
Bacon rolls and tea, okay for me
This was my job
This was my life
No time for a lover
No time for a wife.

The work was endless,
Long hours, long days
But always exciting,
No better ways.
All cash, no tax

A really free life.
I kept on going
With nearly fifty shops
We can all do it,
We just need to try.
Don't be lazy, it's not crazy
don't just get by.
It was only a stall,
But oh, what a ball.

QUICK PUNCH

First punch he countered
hit him in the ribs
then, right hook
And cut his eye
They fixed it

He went down, no sound
No more light, no right or wrong
It wasn't long, it was over
The fight

PEOPLE ALWAYS LET YOU DOWN

They're never there when you're around
They just never seem to care
When I think that someone's there
And you make it very clear
They always seem to let you down
Turn away or play around
Let you know the reason why
Which doesn't satisfy
Just wants to make you cry.
People always let you down.

The impact of the kiss
The very thing you miss
And racing through my brain
Causing so much pain
People always let you down.

For an instant, I don't care
Because there's no one there
And if could I would
Take a chance on life,
Be alone no more, but
people always let you down.

FALLING LEAVES

Squirrels darting up gnarled tree trunks
Collecting acorns from the dew-kissed grass
Lakes glistening with reflections
Of autumnal sunlight
Leaves were falling
Cinnamon timbre, mustard yellows, mellow greens and burnt orange
So many shades and hues
As a new page turns and change happens before our eyes.
Crunching through the dried leaf litter
Breathing in the crisp damp air,
As winter's fingers start to tap
I trudge up to my cabin in the hills
A solitary existence
Light a fire, read, and drink a glass of wine
Gradually falling asleep to the ticking clock
Tiredness overtaking me
Cradling me in her winged embrace.

WHY DO WE KILL EVERYTHING?

Why do we cage the bears that should be free
Kill millions of animals
For what?
Hamburgers?
Desecrate the forests,
build weapons that could destroy the earth
Still start wars
For what?
Is the chaos and destruction worth the cost?
Its greed and power
What do we need?
Oxygen, food, a roof – maybe?
Wants not necessities fulfilled
Suffocated with gizmos, toys and junk
Ending up in landfill, buried forever
Our souls scattered in plastic graveyards.

FRAUD

Mobile phone, on your own
Fraudsters, hackers stealing what you have earned
A thief is watching, always peeping
There is no relief
TikTok, Twitter – all hard hitters
Spying on your moves
Unique password, spinning out of gear
Creating tension, insecurity,
So intense, be on your guard
Do we chuck our phones, go back to paper?
Worry later, writing letters
Buy with cash, get a stash
Pay by cheques, use your landline
But, could not text, send an email?
Social chit-chat would all go back in time
Softer, safer, slower pacer
Why the speed? Take a few more days
Get there in the end
But what the hell
Should we bend and go without
the technics, back to basics, more solid ground
Dark Net, bad bet
All the porn,
Go back to records
Is it progress or regression?
A mere stitch in time
Is it great?
Is it all so fine.

NEWS

Heard the news
Same old views
Depressing reporting
Retrogressing, distorting
Such old rope
We're not all dopes.

Bad news sells
Rings our bells
Keeps us on our feet
Could there be war?
Possible strikes?
Inflation running high
Money short
Harder times
All bad news
Nothing very good
We fight the fight
Where is Robin Hood?

If nothing's good
And it's all bad
What is the point in going on?
We could go home
Sit in a chair
Not watch the news,
Not hear the views.

REHAB

Keep them all in
It won't be a sin
I'm in a rage
In a cage
Let me out
Fulfil all my dreams
Don't feel ready
Or even steady
I would leave and score
Possibly more
Could stay here
Bear it longer
Try to survive

But I'm in a rage
In a cage
Not alone, but weak and angry
Got to get straight
Try to be sober
Shivering and cold
Feeling sick, lick my wounds,
Go cold turkey,
I just can't do that
Still feel the rage and anger,
Try to weep
Get some sleep
Getting older, look so drawn
I am a fool
Just a pawn.

A MONK'S CALL

In my cell
I feel at peace
A haven
A place of rest
To contemplate
To be alone
No outside fuss

A place of trust
A womb
A nest
A home at last.

S.S.D.D.

It's not my scene,
Feeling groovy,
Far out and solid, (very squalid)
Swinging dodgy, she's my bird
(Shhhh... not a word)
Turkey down the line, (waste of time)
Greenies, half a dollar, (half a crown)
Give us a tanner, FAB, way out
Collar felt, nice one Cyril
Like my bloomers (called that at school)
Spotted dick, (not what you think),
Prawn cocktail, steak diane,
That's not HIP
Rozzers, Bobbies, and the Fuzz
With a whistle, now that's no buzz,
Reefers, puff and L.S.D. getting
High (oh my my), good grief
'Ding dong' I say, politically correct,
not circumspect.
Trendy, (not so cool)
Back doubles (kids don't get it)
Get the map out, find a
phone box, dustmen, clippies,
road sweepers, rag and bone men

You are sexy, (now you're hot), bit of

a boy, (now a shagger), bit of a
goer, (could have been slower), banging, horny
(very corny), gay as happy, moving on
What went wrong? Can you dig it?
Cool for cats, her indoors
Psychedelic, is that right?
Good night!

MY ROBOT

There are all kinds of robots
Ones that walk
Ones that talk
Some are fantastic but made of plastic
Some are wood, can be really good
No none as good as my robot
My robot isn't like any other
He isn't tall but isn't small
He's not quite blue
Not quite grey
He came from a store a long way away
But all that matters is he's my robot

My robot is my friend
Not like any other
He always wants to listen, wants to play
Never to be put away
Sometimes at night when I'm scared
I'm glad I have him in my bed
He guards the door, an eye on the floor
I'm so happy he's my robot.
When I hear mum say, "It's show and tell day,"
There's no question in my mind who I need to find
Come on friend, off we go
It's you and me, me and you.
He's, my robot.

ANY WAR 1

Another day of fighting
Another day of blood
I often feel like crying
Or dying in the mud.
Death all around me
My sword in my hand.
I don't want this to continue
for even more bloody land.

Maybe wake up tomorrow
and find peace at last
But it's so unlikely
we're living in the past.
We cannot walk,
We cannot talk,
Just murder one more man
We don't even know him.
maybe he has a wife
a home he dearly loves
But we just chop his head off
hoping that it's right.
Can we advance much further?
maybe see the light
Or just keep on killing
this endless futile fight.

Soldiers just take orders
do what they are told
Some don't get much older
ten days, most are corpses
Ashes on the ground.
Life has no real value
When you're fighting for the land
But I just stand here
My sword in my hand.

ANY WAR 2

Sloping figure
Hand on the trigger
Maybe later
Used to be a waiter
Now I'm in a war
Fighting for the law.
It's all so raw,
Killing and more
The war is still raging
We're killing civilians
I just want some peace
A final release.

The horror of war
I know what I've seen
Who had I been?
Could have been a contender
Or maybe a vendor
Gun on my shoulder
Wish I was bolder
Wish I was older.
If I last much longer
With the fear and the anger
The shots and explosions
Missiles and bombs
For a bit more land

In my own hand
Without us this couldn't be
The soldiers, the airmen
The killing machine.

A bullet with my name on
Will reach me soon
Maybe tomorrow
Maybe at noon.

VAMPIRES

Suck on energy
Suck on blood
Communicate with bats eat rats
Sleep all day
Roam at night, hate the light
Live for ever, the endless quest
Still need a nest and time to rest

It's in us all if we awake it
We drain those around us
At times charming and then alarming
We are old and grey
but covert as we change our looks
Underground in dusty books
Will not be seen eating little
The living dead, love the red

We know who we are but no longer care
bare our teeth
Feel the earth, sniff our foe
As we enslave those who reach out for us,
on the street on a bus,
careful not to get involved
Remember you've been told.

THE FLYER

The spitfire took off
climbed to cruising height
fully loaded reflecting the light
He met her two months ago
last night they kissed
the love that he missed
He was no longer the boss
he now could know loss
Before he had nothing
not a soul to care
Why did he give himself
now all had changed with her out of range
He loved her and she he
His existence could end in a wink
But now he cared
Now he dared
Now he shared
Someone to lose
A love, a muse
But he was in a war
fighting for more
his love was greater
than his fear of later
He shuddered, the bullets hit the wing
He saw the smoke
He all but choked
I'll never know
As he thought of her
And fell below.

LAURENCE

Was my brother
Five years older than me
We worked together many years
And together faced many fears
His life was short at sixty-three
Died so fast, brain aneurism
Like he was shot
Assassinated, dead in minutes
He was such a loss
He was my bro, my friend
My anchor, the one I trusted
Spent so much time together
When he went, passed away

Passed over to where who knows, to somewhere great
Spiritual I hope
So much was on me and so
quickly, nobody to talk to
No advice, I had to make
all decisions alone, the buck
now stopped with me only.
I miss him so much
I felt abandoned, lost, alone
Felt it deeply in my bones.

Where do they go?

"From the country no man has returned from "
Do they go to heaven, hell, nirvana, or do they not exist?
I think not! Or do they watch
Over our shoulders guide us
Through our labours?

We knew each other so well
Read each other's minds - twins
In many ways, although such
Short days. I wish he was
With me now even for one
Day, so much to discuss, to share,
So rare, I felt like part of
My body had fallen away when he went,
Believed time would heal,
Really it hasn't, it's like it was yesterday, losing a sibling is not
The same as a parent, it hits much harder,
You know you're next, whenever that will be,
Let's wait let's see, it could be you
It could be me.

LEO

Leo is my son
left when he was young
everything went wrong
but now he's back
in the fight.

He's sixteen, great looking boy
worried about his height
but unimportant, not right
he could be a star, or might
work in a bar
a model and a soldier
we'll see as he gets older

Hard time for him
not a boy, not a man
but he'll find his way
maybe a year, maybe a day
he'll know what he needs
know how to lead
Leo Bloom, a literate name
who knows what he'll be
let's wait and see
I hope he won't be me.

DUDLEY

He was a good and kind guy
He was a fine friend
He phoned me and said "Hey what's up?"
I said "Nothing, I'm good"
And then he said "yeah, but what's up?"
He said, "I hate my parents"
He was 41, his parents were kind and considerate
He owned a mews house in central London
Had money, was a chartered surveyor
But he was strange
Used to come to my place and walk in circles
Never sitting, walking, pacing, racing
Had a therapist, she never seemed to help him
Was on strong meds, lived alone
Eating crisps and coca cola
He only eats out
He went to Australia, came back paranoid
Telling me "They are all after us!"
"You as well"
I placated him and tried to help
One night I got a call from him
I did not respond
The next morning, he was dead
He never wanted to be here
He hung himself, he had gone
I miss him.

BOATS

The blue boats slept under their covers
It was winter
They did not move
Settled in the middle of the lake
Not awake
It looked surreal
As they sat there all alone
Waiting for better times, better weather
To feel the sun beating down on their oars
Folk rowing and laughing as they skimmed through the water
But that was not now, they looked peaceful, unmoved, untouched.
The paint flaking beneath the canvas covers
Soon it would change
They would come alive
Survive the cold and snow
Once more to be set free
Not roped together
Enduring the weather

The boats lie there all alone
Unused, frozen by their aloofness
They seem to be waiting for the winter to pass
Waiting to come alive again

To feel their oars skimming the lake
Over the wake
But they sit there
Under their covers
Almost asleep
Suspended in time
Until the sun touches the blue wood
And warms every fibre of life.

AMAZON CHRISTMAS

Online buying is the new
Santa Claus, no chimneys,
No soot, no reindeer, no sleighs,
just click and pay
presents are delivered,
no trekking round stores
poor old Santa, out of a job.
What will he do?

Maybe develop his own website,
or deliver by reindeer or drones,
he will have to update,
Don't wait – Santa.com!
Online, it's fine,
he won't have to visit the whole world.
Every house, every home, every flat
it's the only way, no sleigh.

BLAH BLAH

They're always moaning
Always groaning,
finding many flaws
The doors don't close
The dogs are barking
Nothing really works

If asked it's all okay
They answer, 'yes, it's fine'
and then whine!
Why don't they say
something when they're here
say something new
not go away
and write a blog,
frightened to say what's wrong
Why do they wait so long?
We really care,
why don't they share?

ALONE

I have done something.
wracked with regret
An assassin that shoots the bodyguard, not the president
More than a slip
Bad it is
Should I be sad?
No point!
It is done
To regret it
Why should I?

Alone I am
Cold I am
But alive I am
This is living with all its pain
It's insane
But I did it.

CAREFREE

To be aware
To have no cares
To be away
For years and days
To live for life
Not work and strife
I do declare
We must not dare
For if we doze
We'd decompose
Or would we flourish like a rose
Who knows?

TEN

Letters on my fingers
Numbers on my hands
Words connecting all the time
Then all must be found

Understand concussion,
Not fulfilling what we see
Generating, bedazzling, visions
Puzzlement, everything
In revolution
A silhouette of adaptation
of the truth. O.C.D.
Feels so good yet drives you mad,
along this endless quest.
Hey just
STOP IT!

CLOTHES

I remember the smells,
the acetate, the clear plastic bags, so pungent
The hangers, the rails,
patterns and tickets, sizes too big, too small
Cloth and clothes, dresses and jackets,
Trousers and suits,
Coats and collars, colours and cuffs
Flares and tartan, crepe and chiffon
So many styles
The need to look different
Original
An out of date style has no value at all
We tried to be trendsetters, in all the shops
"Swinging clothes for swinging chicks"
So dated, overrated, the cycle is still the same
It just goes on and on and on
Never ending
Just re-trending.

EATING OUT

Like feeding a very large animal,
with an insatiable appetite
you feed them
Then again
Seven days a week,
so many items from salt and pepper to toilet rolls
So much to do
Hey clean the loo
Opening, closing
Emptying the trash, bank the cash
it never ends, never bends.

The waiters are ill,
the chef is late or drunk
Now multiply it by ten
People say do I miss it?
No, I don't, not at all
Thankless, silver service
they all complain,
Take away again
but the animal has woken,
Feed me, feed me, fill me up.
It never ends, it never bends.

MIST

The mist concealed the light
Confused the time of day
It all seemed so serene
As it crept along the bay
All seemed so still
As put on hold
Along the empty beach
and extending to the empty reach
All alone - no voice, no wind
No sound to complicate the way.

SHE'S NOT THERE

You have gone
no longer there
no cross to bear
no eggshells
to be trodden on, stifle all I care
too upset, don't defend
don't be affected
becoming such a bore, sensitive to the core,
the repetition
just talk louder, so I can hear you
could it be worse?
shout and scream
create a drama
without this fuss
it could be calmer
choosing to interact with all
the rows
time will tell
thoughts I couldn't express
no more rage
disengaged, becoming
older, feeling
colder anyway
she was not there.

RAINBOW DAYS

From Genesis to Punk and Human League
From all the world they came and went
Deadheads and more…
It was eerie as I walked in
Floor covered in posters
Thousands of empty red velvet seats
Backdrop Tommy, bedraggled and torn
There was a chilling air
as if all the energy had died
I felt all the crowds
Who had come over the years and had been elated
By what they had experienced
By what they had seen
But now old ticket stubs strewn about
Ghostly and strange
but compelling and so telling.

JO JO'S

All the girls, but not really
Chicks with dicks
Soho with all its glam
Pretty but deep voices
Stockings, minis, wigs,
Duality with all its confusions
The show,
Ruby doing her stuff
Banquettes and barbettes
A crazy but exciting illusion
Fannies and trannies,
A place to get lost in.
Champagne, smoke and chicken in the basket,
Or on the floor.
Men questioning their feelings
Not knowing where to look
Mitzie and Barbie and Ruby and
All the babes that wanted change.

THE END

We're at the end
The cliff's edge
Nowhere to go
No more to show

It could be hard
To adjust again
It could be marred
To run the show
As we get by
With every inch
With every pinch
In our supply.

We can still have fun
Enjoy the days
Without someone with
all the praise
It's just the end
A new fresh start
Remembering it all when…

SOHO

Spent so many years there,
The clubs and pubs,
All the sleeze
Working girls, trans and touts
Doorman, neon lights attacked your eyes
Bar Italia, Raymond Review
Old bill checking capacity
Clip joints, porno cinemas,
Men in macs some in suits
At 3am it was empty
Quiet, real, surreal, peaceful, good time to think
Earning when all were asleep
No sound, no peek
A smart girl approached
I told her the time
She offered me sex
I was surprised
Soho was so special in the early hours
It was decadent, hedonistic
Full of temptation
Now it's cool, mainstream
The Box, JoJo's reopening
Become more open to all
It was the only area at the time that was different
Inane, insane
Now sex shops, LGBTQ bars, becoming global
Same as all the other streets
Greedy landlords, no longer cheap
It's all done
was somewhere to run
not so much fun.

SHADY PEOPLE

Sat at my table in the club,
he joined me
used to getting his own way
his play, missed bets, veiled threats
A bad guy dealer selling dreams

Without him clubs would not survive
clientele would disappear.

Do I want a share?
No, not good, not right, not bright.
He stared at me unblinking
It would happen anyway
If I agreed or not
Not a good life
Will not keep a wife, sham, a front.
He got up with disdain,
It was a good try,
he looked me in the eye
but did not say goodbye.

A.I.

Soon our brains will change
Not make decisions
Not remember phone numbers,
Not read a map
All such a trap.

They will choose our dates
Select our mates
Make our investments
Undermine the will
Robotic girls, robotic boys,
using the toys
We will not trust our choice
AI will decide
We're here for the ride.
We'll become more like computers
Not the reverse
It's all a mess
Our brains become less
Automatons, VR
Is this what we want?
Reducing memory
The machine knows better.
We won't write a letter
It's all control
Told how we feed

And what we need
On Instagram and Twitter
It must be as good as it should
Your voice
Your choice
Time will tell full of charm
It should sound the alarm
Write a report
Time to abort.

BLACKBUSHE

Best concert of all,
A year to set up,
250000 people in one day,
babies born, toilets overflowed,
a river of yellow, delay towers, brochures,
concessions, bridges built and more.
Tom Petty, Joan Armatrading and
Greg Lake, what a day, but when
Dylan hit the stage,
wow what a unique moment in time.

STARS

Meeting rock stars, actors, footballers
politicians, DJs, writers and journalists
Interviews - asking questions,
Yes, it's so exciting
A wired life.
They don't care
Just tell us more,
spill the beans
Fragile egos
Needing to know how great they are, propped at the bar
Have another drink you won't care
Did they like you, did they not?
Are they rare, who cares?
We're all the same
Some make it, some blame
Another act, another play
If lucky, an extra day.

LIVES

I knew the time had come to pass
when fear and love could break like glass
Feelings that were built to last
had withered in the hand of past
Moments I have held today
wilt in time and pass away.

FINAL FREEHOLD

Do we really own it
Or is it just leased?
After we are done
Underneath the earth
Do they feed on us forever?
Cash and tax to be found.

We are only here a short time
And pay, and pay, and pay,
But is it really over,
As bills are on the way?
It's not any different,
Just another day.

The end could be celebrated,
Not mourning and so sad,
Maybe to a better place,
Which actually is not so bad.
Fulfil our dreams, hear the playing
of the band
As we wind our soulful journey
To the promised land.

The Grim Reaper, he's no sleeper,
He's knocking on the wall
Whether old, tall or small

He stops you in mid flow
and you really have to go
So, let's be bright, uninvolved

Seeing gravestones, she died,
So young, he lived longer
He was stronger,
It all appears foretold
Do not fret or bother
We have reached the
Final Freehold.